Health
SCARE

Why 98% of potential medical malpractice
victims never receive compensation

"Take off the blinders of institutional
thinking". Dr. David Eifrig – retired eye
surgeon. (52)

Health
SCARE

Why 98% of potential medical malpractice
victims never receive compensation

John A. McKiggan

WORD ASSOCIATION PUBLISHERS
www.wordassociation.com
1.800.827.7903

Printed in the United States of America.

ISBN: 978-1-59571-679-8

Designed and published by

Word Association Publishers
205 Fifth Avenue
Tarentum, Pennsylvania 15084

www.wordassociation.com
1.800.827.7903

Table of Contents

What Some of Our Readers and Clients Have Said......7

"Who Are You and Why Should I Listen to You?".......9

"Why Did You Write This Book?"......................11

I Am Not Allowed to Give
    Legal Advice in this Book! 15

How Often Does Medical Malpractice Happen? 17

"What is Medical Malpractice?" 21

Consent to Medical Treatment 23

The Burden of Proof.................................27

"What Do I Have to Prove to Win My Case?"..........29

"Are Canadian Medical Malpractice
    Claims More Difficult than in the
    United States?" 35

Canada's Cap on Compensation for
    "Pain and Suffering".............................39

How Is My Claim For Compensation Calculated?......41

Compensation for Fatal Injuries 49

Top Ten Reasons Why 98% of Canadian
    Malpractice Victims Receive No Compensation....53

Doctors Disciplinary Complaints.....................63

"How Do I Find a Qualified
    Medical Malpractice Lawyer?" 67

"How Do I Find Out Who Is Good In My Area?" 69

What Happens After You Decide On A Lawyer? 73

What Do I Do For You in a
    Medical Malpractice Claim? 75

Tasks in a "Typical"
    Medical Malpractice Claim 77

Altered Medical Files:
    What happens when the records
    have been tampered with? 81

The Legal Process in
    Medical Malpractice Cases........................85

The Discovery Examination is the Key
    to a Successful Malpractice Claim 87

The Defence Medical Exam 93

Other Types of Defence
    Medical Examinations...........................103

The GAF Scale in a Nutshell........................109

Nine Tips to Help Prepare
    for your D.M.E.................................113

"So How Long Does
    All of This Take?" 115

Why Should You Hire Me?..........................117

What Cases Do I Not Accept? 119

What Cases Will I Accept? 125

What Some of Our Readers and Clients Have Said

"I found *The Consumer's Guide to Medical Malpractice Claims* most helpful. I would definitely recommend the Guide to anyone seeking information; it was very informative, factual and easy to read. I would certainly recommend the Guide to anyone wondering if they have grounds for a medical malpractice lawsuit." –Lynn Butler

"John thanks a lot, you deserve to be congratulated. Without you and Ron I would have a big zero dollars. We would have never thought of a lawsuit against the doctors and hospital. Therefore I have X number of reasons to thank you. I would also like to thank your staff that worked behind the scenes. Thank them for me; you all did a great job!" –Maurice D. re: 3.8 million dollar medical malpractice claim.

"Paul and I found you very professional and you made us feel like people. That is not an easy attribute to find in someone.
John, you did a great job and I feel you took Paul's brain injury and his challenges into account when speaking with us which means a lot to us. You were very professional while taking into account we have feelings and you always kept us informed about how the claim was going." –Pam R. Halifax Nova Scotia. Re: Serious personal injury claim.

"I am aware of all of the work John McKiggan and his firm have put in on Davey 's behalf and I have no doubt that we would not have been able to get this settlement for Davey if it weren't for John's efforts." —Heidi Paul: Mom and litigation guardian for Davey Paul re: $2.88 million dollar medical malpractice settlement.

"Who Are You and Why Should I Listen to You?"

My name is John McKiggan. I am one of the founding partners of Arnold Pizzo McKiggan, Trial Lawyers. I limit my work to serious personal injury claims, medical malpractice cases and representing survivors of childhood sexual abuse.

My practice is dedicated to providing *peace of mind* to persons who have been seriously injured or to family members who have lost loved ones. While each case is different, and past results cannot be used to predict future success, I can tell you that I have been privileged to help my clients and their families recover millions of dollars in compensation in serious injury claims.

I have been honored by my fellow trial lawyers by being elected President of the Atlantic Provinces Trial Lawyers' Association. I have written papers and presented lectures in Nova Scotia, New Brunswick, Ontario and Singapore on various issues pertaining to sexual abuse litigation, personal injury law, and institutional liability to a variety of groups including the Nova Scotia Barristers Society Continuing Education Lecture Series, the Canadian Bar Association, The Canadian Institute, and the Atlantic Provinces Trial Lawyers' Association. I was honoured to be invited to lecture in Singapore at the annual meeting of the International Bar Association.

You can find out more about me and my firm at *www.apmlawyers.com*. Our web site has a lot of useful information on a variety of subjects. Or you can visit one of my Blogs:

www.halifaxpersonalinjurylawyerblog.com,

www.sexualabuseclaimsblog.com, or

www.halifaxmedicalmalpracticelawyerblog.com.

"Why Did You Write This Book?"

To answer that question, I have to tell you a story. My grandfather was a family doctor in a small town. My father was an internal medicine specialist and Chief of Medicine for more than 20 years at a major hospital here in Nova Scotia. Both of them devoted their lives to helping and healing their patients. They were truly great doctors.

The British Medical Journal once surveyed people in 24 countries around the world and asked them: "what makes a good doctor?" The answers included qualities like compassion, understanding, honesty, humanity, competence, commitment, empathy, respect, creativity and a sense of justice. I agree that a good doctor should be all of these things. But I would add two more requirements; a good doctor is someone who genuinely likes people and has an innate ability to help heal them. My grandfather and my father had all of these traits.

Growing up I had a tremendous amount of respect for the work that my father did and I planned to follow in his footsteps. I studied pre-med for my undergraduate degree. I wrote the medical school entrance exams. I graduated with a science degree with majors in Biology and Anatomy. I was ready to move on to medical school.

But I spent some time talking with some of my fellow students who were also planning on attending medical school. When I asked them why they wanted to become a doctor, a common answer was that they wanted to make a lot of money.

That made me ask myself why I wanted to become a doctor. I asked myself if I had what it took to be a truly great doctor. I decided that I wanted to help people, but I wasn't convinced I had the ability to heal them.

But I realized that most of the qualities shared by great doctors: compassion, understanding, honesty, humanity, competence, commitment, empathy, respect, creativity and a sense of justice, were also traits shared by great lawyers.

So I went to law school, and after graduating I have devoted my career to trying to help people who truly need help, people looking for fairness, people who need justice.

That is why I do medical malpractice litigation and that is why I wrote this book. To provide information to people who have been seriously injured as a result of medical malpractice. To help people who have been betrayed by the person or persons that they had to trust the most, their doctor, their nurse, their health care provider.

Every research study that has been done about medical malpractice claims has concluded that **most victims of medical malpractice never contact a lawyer or file a claim.**

You may not actually have the grounds for a medical malpractice claim, but you do need to have certain important information to know if you have a **potential claim** and what you need to do to protect your rights if you have been a victim of medical malpractice. I wrote this book so that people who may have suffered a loss as a result of medical malpractice can have this information, for free.

Frankly, this method of talking to you also saves me time. I've packed a ton of information into this book and it would typically take me 6 or 7 hours to explain to you face to face. At my normal hourly rate of $400.00 that's more than $2000.00 worth of information to help you understand the issues involved in medical malpractice litigation.

Providing this information to you, free, in this book saves me the hours of time that it would take each day just to talk to all of the new clients who call me.

Rather than cut you short on the phone, writing this book gives me a chance to tell you what you need to know so that you can decide if you have a medical malpractice claim that may be worth pursuing in court. Even if I do not accept your case, I would like you to be educated about the process.

Most lawyers want you to make an appointment in order to get the information that I write about in this book. I believe that you should be able to have this information, right now, and without any pressure.

I Am Not Allowed to Give Legal Advice in this Book!

I can offer you suggestions and help educate you about the issues involved in medical malpractice claims, but please do not construe anything in this book to be legal advice until you have agreed to hire me AND I have agreed, in writing, to accept your case.

I cannot and will not accept every case.

Because I value personal service, I do not accept every case I am asked to take on—I couldn't—there are simply too many.

I am selective about the cases I accept because I want to ensure that my clients cases have the best chance of success.

Hiring a lawyer to represent you is an important decision that should not be taken lightly. I hope that this book will help make that decision easier.

How Often Does Medical Malpractice Happen?

You may have a medical malpractice claim if you have been injured as a result of a preventable error or negligent care while receiving medical treatment.

A famous study by Harvard Medical School determined that over half of all injuries caused by medical mismanagement (in other words, not caused by the patient's initial injury or disease) were preventable, and another quarter of those incidents were caused by negligence.

A report published in the May 25, 2004 edition of the Canadian Medical Association Journal entitled: "The Canadian Adverse Events Study: the incidence of adverse events in hospital patients in Canada" confirmed the findings of similar studies in the United States, Australia, the United Kingdom, Denmark and New Zealand.

THE CANADIAN STUDY CONCLUDED:

- As many as 24,000 patients die each year due to "adverse events" (doctors code words for a bad result or a mistake).

- 87,500 patients admitted annually to Canadian acute care hospitals experience an adverse event.

- 1 in 13 adult patients admitted to a Canadian hospital encounter an adverse event.

- 1 in 19 adults will potentially be given the wrong medication or wrong medication dosage.

- 37% of adverse events are "highly" preventable.

- 24% of preventable adverse events are related to medication error.

A report by the Canadian Institute for Health Information (CIHI) indicated that nearly one quarter of Canadian adults (5.2 million people) reported that they, or a member of their family, had experienced a "preventable adverse event," in other words, a medical error.

For example, fifteen years ago I represented the family of a wife and mother who died suddenly, shortly after taking medication that had been given to her by her family doctor. Her family doctor had been treating her for many years for asthma. The medication the doctor prescribed was very dangerous when taken by anyone on asthma medication.

The family doctor was either not aware of the dangerous side effects of the medication he prescribed, or he had forgotten that his patient had been taking asthma medication for many years.

As a result of this completely preventable medical error, a husband lost his wife of 20 years, and their two daughters lost the love and companionship of their mother.

"What is Medical Malpractice?"

MEDICAL MALPRACTICE CAN HAPPEN IN MANY WAYS:

- If your doctor did not have your informed consent to perform a medical procedure that caused you an injury (I discuss what informed consent is in a later chapter).

- If your doctor was negligent, and the negligence caused your injury (I explain how you prove negligence in a later chapter).

- Medical malpractice can also involve negligence by other health care providers like nurses, chiropractors, ambulance attendants and paramedics, and hospital staff like x-ray technicians and lab personnel.

- Medical malpractice can be caused by an institution (like a hospital) not having proper policies and safety procedures in place to protect patients against injury.

- If you or a loved one have suffered a serious injury (or fatality) it is prudent to get advice from an experienced medical malpractice lawyer to determine if the injury or death may have been caused by medical malpractice.

Consent to Medical Treatment

Everyone has the legal right to decide what can be done with his or her own body. This is called autonomy. Because of this legal right, your doctors need your permission, (the legal term is consent) before they can treat you.

WHAT IS INFORMED CONSENT?

You can only give valid permission if you are provided with all the information that is necessary to make a decision about the proposed medical treatment. It is not acceptable for your doctor to simply ask if he or she has your permission to perform a medical procedure.

You must be able to understand the reasonable and foreseeable consequences of giving permission (consent), or not giving permission, for the medical procedure.

It is generally accepted that in order to provide proper permission for medical treatment your doctor must explain:

- The nature of the proposed medical procedure;

- The reasonable alternatives to the proposed medical procedure; and

- The relevant risks, benefits, and uncertainties related to each alternative.

Your permission or consent may be expressed in words or implied by your actions. For example, when you are undergoing a surgical procedure your doctor will usually get you to sign a consent form as part of the consent process to confirm your permission to perform the medical procedure.

Any medical procedure that is performed without proper informed consent is deemed to be an assault. The doctor who performed the medical procedure will be responsible for any injury suffered by the patient as a result of the medical procedure.

Unfortunately, it is very difficult to win medical malpractice cases involving allegations of informed consent. Often the question of whether the risks were properly explained to the patient boils down to the doctor's word against the patient.

In most of the reported medical malpractice cases across Canada, judges and juries tend to favour the doctors word, unless there is clear evidence to support the patient's version of events.

Therefore, it is important to document the consent process by making notes of any discussions that you have with your doctor before you undergo a medical procedure. Particularly any discussion you have with your doctor about the risks, benefits and alternatives of the proposed medical procedure.

The Burden of Proof

THE PLAINTIFF (YOU) BEARS THE BURDEN OF PROVING YOUR CASE.

Most people have heard the term: "proof beyond a reasonable doubt". That is NOT the burden that applies in medical malpractice claims for compensation; it is the burden that applies to criminal prosecutions.

In a personal injury compensation claim you bear the burden of proof: "on the balance of probabilities". In other words, is it more likely than not that the doctor was negligent and that the negligence caused your injuries.

The easiest way to think about this is to consider a pair of scales. All the evidence FOR your claim is placed on one side of the scale. All the evidence AGAINST your claim is placed on the other side of the scale.

As long as the scales tip to the side FOR your claim, even a little bit, then you have met the burden of proof on the balance of probabilities.

"What Do I Have to Prove to Win My Case?"

There are several things that you have to prove in order to win your medical malpractice case:

STANDARD OF CARE:

People are not expected to be perfect. Just because someone makes a mistake does not necessarily mean the mistake was negligence. But sometimes a mistake is so obvious it is considered to be negligent.

Doctors and nurses are expected to use reasonable care and judgment when treating patients. Doctors and nurses are expected to meet the standard of care expected of a reasonably competent doctor or nurse. If they fail to meet the standard of care, that's negligence.

You will need expert evidence to show what standard of care is expected of a reasonably competent doctor (or nurse). Doctors in the same specialty as the negligent doctor must be willing to testify that the conduct of the doctor fell below accepted standards. Doctors are not expected to be perfect. But they are expected to be reasonably competent.

ARE THERE DIFFERENT "STANDARDS OF CARE"?

The short answer is, yes. The "standard of care" in medical malpractice cases means the standard that reasonably competent doctors (or health care professionals) have to meet when providing medical care.

But the standard of care may be different depending on the type of medical care you received or where you were treated.

SPECIALISTS HELD TO HIGHER STANDARDS

Medical specialists are held to a higher standard of care than family doctors because of the extensive nature of the medical training they have received. Courts expect specialists who have received additional training to be able to identify, diagnose and treat illnesses and conditions family physicians might not have the education, training or experience to properly treat.

LOCALITY RULE

In some cases, courts have held that where the negligence happens makes a difference to the standard of care expected. In other words, a doctor practicing medicine in a rural hospital that does not have access to an M.R.I. machine or other sophisticated medical equipment may not be held to the same standard of care as a doctor practicing in a teaching hospital in Vancouver, Montreal, Toronto or Halifax.

"BUSY" DOCTORS DON'T HAVE LOWER STANDARDS OF CARE

However, our courts have specifically rejected arguments made that "busy" family doctors should be held to a lower standard of care than doctors who practice part-time or in a teaching hospital.

WHAT ABOUT MEDICAL STUDENTS?

In many hospitals throughout Canada the primary medical care is provided, not by a specialist, but by medical students who are receiving further training in their medical sub-specialty.

The medical students, called residents, typically spend one, two, three or four years training to become authorized to practice in a particular specialized field of medicine.

If the alleged medical malpractice was committed by medical resident student, should the student be held to the higher standard of care of a medical specialist or the lower standard of care of a general medical practitioner?

Canadian Courts have held that a higher degree of training and experience will raise the applicable standard but a lack of training and experience will not lower the standard.

Therefore, residents studying in specialized fields of medicine will be held to a higher standard of care.

BREACH OF THE STANDARD:

You will need expert evidence to prove that the doctor (or nurse) did not meet the standard expected of a reasonably competent doctor (or nurse).

In other words, did they do something that they should not have done, or did they fail to do something that they should have done?

Making a simple mistake or getting a bad result is not enough – you must prove that it was a significant error which directly led to your injury.

CAUSATION:

Not only must you prove that the doctor (or nurse) breached the standard of care; you must also prove that the breach actually caused your injury.

It is possible that a doctor can be negligent (breach the standard of care), but the negligence isn't what caused the injury

For example, failing to wear surgical gloves during an operation is a breach of the standard of a competent doctor. But it is not likely to have caused you to suffer a stroke during the operation.

On the other hand, failing to wear gloves may very well cause a surgical wound to become infected, leading to serious injury or death.

DAMAGES:

Finally, you have to prove what the financial consequences of the injury has been so that the court can award damages for pain and suffering, and any income loss or medical expenses as a result of your injury.

You will need experts like physical medicine specialists to prove the extent of your injuries; vocational experts to establish how your injuries affect your ability to work; and actuarial or economic experts to calculate your past and future income loss and future pension loss.

"Are Canadian Medical Malpractice Claims More Difficult than in the United States?"

IN A WORD; YES.

Lot's of people have read about large jury awards for personal injury claims in the United States. Sometimes the American jury awards seem to be out of proportion to the injury.

In Canada, court awards are much lower than awards for similar injuries from courts in the United States. Cases that might be successful in the U.S. are simply not economically feasible to pursue in Canada.

Nova Scotia also has some of the most conservative (lowest) awards in Canada for compensation for personal injury claims.

ROLE OF THE C.M.P.A.:

In Canada, most doctors are defended by a single organization, the Canadian Medical Protection Association (the C.M.P.A.).

According to their 2010 annual statement, the C.M.P.A. has two point six nine (2.69) BILLION DOLLARS in assets (money in the bank). The C.M.P.A. uses this money to hire the best experts and lawyers money can buy.

Many victims of serious medical errors cannot work, or have huge expenses for ongoing rehabilitation or medical care.

Against such overwhelming financial odds, Canadian victims of medical malpractice face an almost insurmountable challenge to obtain justice and fair compensation for their injuries.

Remember the Canadian Medical Association Journal study that determined that over 87,000 patients in Canada suffer an adverse event and as many as 24,000 people die each year due to medical errors? That's more than 100,000 potential malpractice claims in Canada every year!

In the last five years, the C.M.P.A. reports only 4524 lawsuits were filed against doctors in Canada: less than 1000 claims per year.

In other words, out of 100,000 potential claims 99% of medical malpractice victims never even filed a claim!

The C.M.P.A. annual reports brag about it's success rate in defending claims brought against doctors. In the past five years, 3089 claims were dismissed or abandoned because the victim or his or her family quit or ran out of money, or died before trial.

SOME FRIGHTENING STATISTICS

- Of the 521 cases that went to trial only 116 resulted in a verdict for the Plaintiff victim. In other words, only twenty-two percent (22%) of medical malpractice plaintiffs actually won their trial.

- For the few victims who won at trial, the median damage award was only $117,000.00.

- In 2009 the C.M.P.A. spent 76 million dollars on legal fees to defend doctors in law suits across Canada.

- Of more than 4000 lawsuits filed against doctors, only two percent (2%) resulted in trial verdicts for the victim.

In other words, ninety eight percent (98%) of potential Canadian medical malpractice victims never received a penny in compensation!

Canada's Cap on Compensation for "Pain and Suffering"

In 1978 in a case known as Teno v. Arnold the Supreme Court of Canada created an additional barrier to recovery for innocent victims who have been injured as a result of someone else's negligence. In the Teno case, the Supreme Court ruled that no matter how seriously injured you are the maximum compensation you can receive for what is commonly referred to as "pain and suffering" is one hundred thousand dollars ($100,000.00).

Taking inflation into account, the cap on pain and suffering awards is currently considered to be slightly more than three hundred thousand dollars ($300,000.00). But the maximum amount is only paid to the most catastrophically injured victims (quadriplegia, paraplegia, severe brain damage and similar injuries).

Even plaintiffs that receive awards that seem large, often never see the amount decided by the judge or the jury. Many awards are drastically reduced on appeal. These reduced or vacated judgments are almost never reported by the media.

How Is My Claim For Compensation Calculated?

WHAT TYPES OF THINGS CAN I RECEIVE COMPENSATION FOR?

The goal of the court in any claim for compensation for personal injuries is to try to put the injured person (or their surviving family members) in the same position that they would have been in if the negligent act had not occurred.

Money can't replace the loss of a loved one or truly compensate for the loss of a limb or a catastrophic injury. But the courts try to provide a fair and reasonable measure of financial compensation to innocent victims who have been injured as a result of the negligence of others.

NON-PECUNIARY DAMAGES:

A non-pecuniary claim is one that does not result in a direct out of pocket financial loss but is still considered to be worthy of compensation. Non pecuniary damages are sometimes referred to as compensation for "pain and suffering" but they cover any non-financial loss.

HOW DO THE COURTS CALCULATE "PAIN AND SUFFERING"?

There is no such thing as a "pain-o-meter". An injured victim can not be hooked up to a machine that prints out the financial value of their pain. What the courts do in determining compensation or pain and suffering is use their experience and discretion to consider how the victim's injuries have limited their ability to function. In other words, how their injuries affect their normal day to day activities and or their ability to work?

The Supreme Court of Canada has placed a cap on the amount of compensation that injured victims can receive for non pecuniary damages for pain and suffering. If you are considering a claim for compensation for non pecuniary damages it is important to have an experienced lawyer assisting you to ensure that you provide all of the relevant information that the courts will consider when assessing your claim for "non-pecuniary damages."

FATAL INJURIES:

In claims by family members for the loss of a loved one, the courts will assess compensation for non pecuniary damages for "loss of care, guidance and companionship."

How much the family members are entitled to receive under this heading depends a great deal on the facts of each case. However, the courts in each province have established ranges of compensation that they will award to certain family members.

Compensation awards in Canada for loss of care, guidance and companionship are much lower than similar awards in the United States.

I go into more detail about fatal injury claims in a later chapter.

PECUNIARY DAMAGES:

A pecuniary claim is one that has (or will) result in a direct out of pocket financial loss. For example, the cost of paying for medical treatment is a pecuniary loss. Past and future income loss is also a pecuniary loss.

COMPENSATION FOR INCOME LOSS:

Your injuries may have caused you to miss time from work. In the case of serious injuries, you may have missed a great deal of time from work or you may never be able to work again.

The Courts consider claims for loss of income two ways:

PAST LOSS OF INCOME:

- You are entitled to be compensated for your actual income loss up to the date of settlement or trial. Usually this loss is one that is capable of being calculated fairly accurately.

FUTURE LOSS OF INCOME:

- If your injuries prevent you from being able to work in the future you are also entitled to be compensated for that loss. Claims for future loss of income can be difficult to calculate with precision. No one knows, for sure, what the future will hold.

- When valuing a claim for future loss of income the court will have to consider whether your injuries will prevent you from being able to work for two months, two years or forever. Calculating claims for future income loss usually requires us to retain the services of an actuary or an economist who are experts in calculating past and future income loss claims.

DIMINISHED EARNING CAPACITY:

In some cases, the evidence may prove that your injuries will result in a future loss of income. However, we may no be able to calculate exactly what that loss will be. In those cases the courts may consider awarding you compensation for what is called "diminished earning capacity."

Everyone's ability to work is an asset. In other words, your physical abilities, your education, training and experience are all assets that allow you to earn an income. If any or all of those abilities have been limited or reduced to some extent by your injuries you may be entitled to an award for diminished earning capacity.

Again, this type of claim usually requires us to hire experts to calculate exactly how your injuries have reduced your ability to work and to what extend your ability to earn income has been diminished.

LOSS OF VALUABLE SERVICES:

Sometimes your injuries prevent you from being able to perform certain household duties that you were able to do the accident. For example, I have had many clients whose injuries prevent them from being able to perform their normal housekeeping chores. We have made claims to compensate my clients for the expense of hiring housekeepers to come into their home to do laundry, wash their dishes, make their beds, etc. In other words, to perform the housekeeping duties that my clients normally performed before they were injured.

I have had clients who were no longer able to perform their household maintenance activities. We have submitted claims to cover the cost of mowing their lawn, shoveling their side walk, and generally maintaining their home.

In other words, loss of valuable services covers the normal day to day physical activities that a home owner has to engage in to maintain their home and their property.

I represented a single Mom who suffered a spinal cord injury and was confined to a wheelchair. We were able to recover compensation for her for the cost of hiring a child care worker to come into her home to help care for her two young children until she was able to care for her children on her own.

If your injuries prevent you from being able to perform a physical duty, chore or activity that you normally were able to perform before you were injured, the court will consider compensating you for the actual financial costs of hiring someone to perform those duties.

COST OF MEDICAL CARE:

Many of my clients who have been seriously injured have significant on going medical expenses for physiotherapy, massage therapy, chiropractic treatment, medication, in home nursing care and so on.

In the case of catastrophic injuries, the lifetime cost of ongoing medical care can be enormous. For example, in a recent medical malpractice case we represented the family of a child who had been severally brain injured The lifetime cost of providing ongoing medical care to the child was calculated by our experts to be $2,113,373.00.

OTHER LOSSES:

There are other areas that the courts will consider when awarding compensation to injured victims. It is important that you have the advice of an experienced personal injury lawyer to ensure that you have identified and provided sufficient evidence to properly calculate all of the losses that you, or your family, will experience as a result of your injury or the death of your loved one.

Compensation for Fatal Injuries

HOW DO YOU PUT A PRICE ON THE LOSS OF A LOVED ONE?

Of course, there is no way to truly place a value on the loss of a loved one due to a fatal injury. Law makers in Canada and the Courts have struggled with the question of how to fairly compensate surviving family members for the loss of a loved one.

Many of us have read news reports of cases in the United States where surviving family members have been awarded huge sums of money for the death of a family member. Unfortunately, the laws in Canada regarding compensation for fatal injuries are very different, and compensation awards rarely reach the levels seen in American cases.

BACKGROUND:

Each province in Canada has laws governing claims for compensation for fatal injuries. The laws allow a claim to be made by the family members of a deceased person where his or her death was caused by the intentional or negligent act of another.

Originally claims for compensation were limited to the monetary losses as a result of the fatal injury, in other words, the actual out of pocket financial loss resulting from the person's death. The law did not take into account non-financial losses like the grief and sorrow experienced by family members or the loss of care, guidance and companionship that the deceased family member might have provided had they not passed away.

Currently, every province in Canada has legislation that allows family members to recover some measure of compensation for the loss of care, guidance and companionship of a deceased family member. It is important to remember that each province has its own specific law with specific rules governing which family members are entitled to make a claim, how the claims are to be assessed, and the amount of damages that can be recovered.

In any claim involving a fatal injury it is important that you speak to an experienced personal injury lawyer to determine which family members are eligible to make a claim for compensation and to ensure that their claim for compensation is properly calculated.

For example, in Nova Scotia claims for loss of care, guidance and companionship can only be brought by parents, grandparents, children and spouses (including common law). Siblings (brothers and sisters) are not entitled to file a claim for compensation.

The amount of the compensation that can be recovered in Nova Scotia depends a great deal on the nature of the relationship and the facts of each particular case. If you are considering filing a claim for compensation for the loss of a loved one it is vitally important that you speak to an experienced personal injury attorney to insure that all of the relevant facts and evidence are provided to the court to ensure that you receive full and fair compensation.

Top Ten Reasons Why 98% of Canadian Malpractice Victims Receive No Compensation

Despite media reports about malpractice lawsuits and awards, according to the most recent C.M.P.A. annual reports, the number of lawsuits against doctors in Canada has dropped "dramatically." In the last ten years, the number of malpractice claims filed against doctors has dropped by almost **fifty percent.**

There are a number of reasons why patients do not recover compensation for injuries suffered while receiving medical care. Most of these reasons stem from general misconceptions about medical malpractice.

It is important for potential malpractice plaintiffs to understand these issues when looking for a lawyer to represent their case.

REASON NUMBER ONE:

PATIENTS DON'T KNOW THEY ARE VICTIMS OF MEDICAL MALPRACTICE:

In Canada roughly seven point five percent (7.5%) of admitted hospital patients suffer some sort of medical error (or "adverse event" to use the doctor's term).

Incredibly, there is no law in Canada that requires doctors or hospitals to report medical errors to patients or their families!

In the vast majority of medical malpractice cases, the fact that a poor medical outcome was caused by malpractice is hidden from the patient.

Every year there are over 100,000 medical errors leading to "adverse events" but only about 1000 lawsuits are filed against doctors each year.

REASON NUMBER TWO:

CANADA'S "LOSER PAYS" RULE:

In Canada, the courts have what is known as a "loser pays" rule. What that means is that, in most cases, the person that loses a lawsuit has to pay some of the legal fees and all the out of pocket expenses of the person that wins the lawsuit.

The theory behind the "loser pays" rule is that it is supposed to discourage frivolous lawsuits. If you know you will have to pay the defendant's legal expenses if you lose, you will think twice before filing a lawsuit that doesn't have merit.

Although the idea of this rule was to discourage frivolous lawsuits, in practice it actually has the effect of discouraging people with legitimate lawsuits from pursuing their claims.

Assume, for example, that you have been seriously injured as a result of medical malpractice. You can't work, your bills are piling up, and you can't pay your mortgage. Then your lawyer tells you that if you file a lawsuit and lose, you might have to pay the defendant doctor or hospital tens of thousands of dollars. What are the chances that you are going to proceed with your lawsuit? Pretty slim, right?

I have had dozens of cases over the years where impartial medical experts have advised me that my client's injuries were the result of medical malpractice. However, the injured patient decided not to file a medical malpractice claim because they were afraid that if they lost the lawsuit, they might be ordered to pay legal costs to the doctor that they had accused of medical malpractice.

The sad fact is that the C.M.P.A., the organization that defends doctors, has almost unlimited financial resources, compared to injured patients who have almost no ability to finance the significant costs of medical malpractice litigation.

That is why I am extremely selective in the medical malpractice cases that I agree to take on. I will not agree to represent a patient in a medical malpractice claim unless I am convinced their claim has merit and that the injured patient has a reasonable chance of successfully recovering compensation for their injuries.

I understand that the decision to file a medical malpractice lawsuit is one of the most important decisions that my clients will ever make. However, most of my clients who have been catastrophically injured as a result of medical negligence literally have no choice. They face huge medical bills and may never be able to work. Filing a medical malpractice claim is the only hope that they have of ever receiving compensation, and justice, for what happened to them.

REASON NUMBER THREE:

NO AUTOPSY WAS PERFORMED:

Remember that you must prove both carelessness on the part of the doctor or nurse and that the carelessness caused the death or injury. In a medical malpractice case that results in death, it is almost impossible to prove the death occurred because of malpractice without an autopsy.

There are many reasons why a person might have died. The problem is that you must prove the one reason they died is because of the negligence of the doctor or nurse.

REASON NUMBER FOUR:

THE CLAIM MAY NOT RECEIVE ENOUGH COMPENSATION TO COVER THE LEGAL EXPENSES OF A TRIAL:

We decline dozens of cases a year where it appears that the doctor was negligent but the resulting injury is not significant enough to justify the enormous expense of a malpractice trial.

For example, we reviewed one case where the patient was given the wrong medication and had a serious allergic reaction. He was violently ill for almost two weeks. He lost time from work as a result. But he had a good recovery.

Even though we thought we could prove the doctor was negligent in prescribing the wrong medication, we determined that the client didn't have a claim that was economically worth pursuing. The costs of the case would likely be greater than the expected recovery.

REASON NUMBER FIVE:

THE PATIENT CAN'T PROVE HIS OR HER INJURY WAS CAUSED BY THE DOCTOR'S OR HOSPITAL'S MISTAKE:

It is very difficult to prove that medical mismanagement (negligence) was the reason why the patient suffered an injury. There are a number of arguments, or defences, that a doctor can raise to avoid being held responsible for victims' injuries.

The five most common defences filed by doctors in malpractice claims are:

1. The injury was an unforeseeable consequence of the medical treatment. For example one client we helped suffered serious injuries as a result of side effects from medication given to him by his doctor. The doctor argued that the side effects were so rare that they were not foreseeable.

2. The injury was caused by the patient not following proper medical advice. For example, in one case we reviewed the patient didn't attend his appoint for a chest x-ray and eventually died from undiagnosed lung cancer.

3. The patient's particular injury was a recognized risk of the procedure and the risk was properly explained to the patient. In other words, the patient gave informed consent to undergo the risks of the procedure.

4. Some other party was responsible for causing the injury. In one case we successfully settled, the doctor argued that the hospital's faulty medical equipment, not the doctor's negligent care, was responsible for my client's serious brain injury.

5. The injury was caused by a previous illness or disease. For example, the doctor may claim that your disabling back pain was not the result of negligent surgery but due to pre-existing arthritis.

REASON NUMBER SIX:

THE PLAINTIFF HAS NOT RETAINED AN EXPERIENCED MEDICAL MALPRACTICE LAWYER:

Medical malpractice litigation is extremely complicated. It requires not only an understanding of the law but of the principles of anatomy, medicine and biomechanics. It has its own special rules and laws.

I believe that it is imperative that you be represented by an experienced medical malpractice lawyer.

REASON NUMBER SEVEN:

THE STATUTE OF LIMITATIONS HAS RUN OUT:

Each Province has its own statute of limitations (time limit) for filing a medical malpractice suit. The length of time may be different in each Province, and the time when the statute starts to run varies as well.

A statute of limitations can begin to run when medical services are rendered, when an injury is discovered (or should have been discovered), or some combination of the two.

One reason that you should consult an experienced medical malpractice lawyer as soon as possible is to determine when the statute of limitations runs out in your case. For example, in Nova Scotia the limitation period is only two years, but if the claim involves a fatality (death) it is just one year.

REASON NUMBER EIGHT:

JURORS HAVE BEEN BIASED BY THE INSURANCE INDUSTRY:

The insurance industry has spent millions of dollars funding "research" to suggest that damage awards for personal injury claims have been increasing out of control. The real facts show that damage awards have not been increasing and insurance companies in Canada have been making record profits. (These facts and other important information can be found in my book: The Consumer's Guide to Car Accident Claims in Nova Scotia.)

This type of propaganda is the reason many provinces in Canada have passed laws limiting recovery for pain and suffering for victims of car accidents.

For example, in Nova Scotia the limit for compensation for a "minor injury" from a car accident is just seven thousand five hundred dollars ($7,500.00). Because of insurance company propaganda, some people mistakenly believe that this cap also applies to medical malpractice claims.

REASON NUMBER NINE:

THE PLAINTIFF IS NOT ABLE TO AFFORD TO HIRE GOOD, QUALIFIED EXPERTS:

You cannot win a medical malpractice case without one or more very qualified medical experts. They can be hard to find. It is becoming increasingly difficult to find doctors who are willing to stand up for what's right. It takes time and money to find the best experts for your case.

In 2009, the CMPA spent **$12 million dollars** to hire experts to defend doctors in malpractice claims.

This is one area where the C.M.P.A. has a tremendous advantage. If they have a case that is particularly bad for their doctor, they can afford to hire as many experts as it takes to get an opinion they can use to defend the doctor. Most patients cannot afford to have several experts look at their case in order to find out which expert will give them the "best" answer.

For example, we were retained to represent a man who was totally and permanently disabled as a result of the side effects of certain medication prescribed to him by his doctor. We retained the services of one of Canada's top experts in the particular medical specialty involved in our client's case.

The expert reviewed the facts of our client's case and gave us an opinion that the defendant doctor was clearly negligent. However, when we provided the expert with the name of our client, and the name of the defendant doctor, she told us she had been retained by the C.M.P.A. the year before and had already given them the same opinion! The claim eventually settled for 3.5 million dollars.

In our search for the best experts to represent our clients' interests we found, purely by luck, one of the experts that the C.M.P.A. had consulted. How many more experts did the

C.M.P.A. consult, and how much money did they spend, in order to get an opinion they could use to defend my client's claim? There is no way to know.

REASON NUMBER TEN:

THE PATIENT CONTRIBUTED TO THE INJURY.

Any negligence on the part of the patient which contributed to the injury will reduce the amount of the damages the victim is entitled to recover. Any carelessness on the part of the patient is balanced against the carelessness of the doctor and damages are apportioned accordingly.

For example, we were asked to review a potential claim where a doctor failed to diagnose a case of lung cancer. The doctor had recommended that the patient get a chest x-ray. The patient forgot to attend the appointment. The expert we retained was of the opinion that the patient's failure to get the x-ray significantly delayed the possibility of getting appropriate treatment that might have saved his life.

.

Doctors Disciplinary Complaints

"ARE THERE ALTERNATIVES TO FILING A LAWSUIT?"

I get several calls a week from patients, of family members of patients, who are concerned about the care that they, or their family member, have received from their doctor or hospital.

In most cases, a careful investigation of the facts reveals that there are no grounds for a medical malpractice claim (in other words, the doctor, hospital or health care worker wasn't negligent) or that there may have been negligence in the patient's care, but the cost of filing a lawsuit would be more than the potential recovery.

Explaining these facts to my clients is one of the more frustrating aspects of being a medical malpractice lawyer. I hate telling patients that I believe there was negligence in the care they received but that I don't think they should pursue a compensation claim.

Sometimes the people that contact me don't want to file a lawsuit. But they tell me: "I don't want the same thing that happened to me happen to anyone else."

COLLEGE OF PHYSICIANS AND SURGEONS

If you are not satisfied with the care that you or your family has received, you can file a complaint with the College of Physicians and Surgeons. Each province has a College of Physicians and Surgeons that is made up of a panel of doctors and lay persons (non doctors) who are responsible for hearing complaints about doctor's conduct and administering discipline.

Discipline can range from something as simple as giving the doctor a warning to as serious as suspending the doctor's license or taking away the doctor's license to practice medicine in that province.

FILE A COMPLAINT

I encourage patients and family members who are concerned about a doctor's conduct to contact the College of Physicians and Surgeons to express their concerns. Often the patients don't follow through with the complaint. I think this is a real mistake.

There are certain doctors who I have received calls about from concerned patients. However, if the patients don't file a complaint with the College of Physicians and Surgeons, there is no way for the College to know about potential concerns regarding the doctor's conduct.

When a patient finally files a complaint the College may not take the complaint as seriously because it is the first complaint received about a particular doctor. The Board members' reasoning may be something like: "Well, we have only received one complaint about his/ her conduct. Lets give the doctor a warning to make sure it doesn't happen again".

On the other hand, if the College has received a half dozen or more complaints about the same doctor they will be more likely to take the complaint seriously and more likely to administer more severe discipline to the doctor.

"WHAT DOES IT COST?"

It doesn't cost anything to file a complaint with the College of Physicians and Surgeons. The complaint can be filed by the patient or by a person on behalf of the patient (spouse, parent, child, friend, lawyer, physician, etc.).

"WHAT INFORMATION DO I NEED TO INCLUDE?"

Complaints to the College must be in writing and must include the following information:

- The patient's name

- The patient's mailing address

- The patient's telephone number

- The patient's MCP number

- The doctor's full name; and,

- The doctor's address.

The College will also require the patient to consent to release of the patient's medical information to the College so that the College can conduct it's investigation. The consent must be from the patient (or the patient's legal representative).

If a doctor has hospital privileges, you can also complain to the appropriate regional health authority.

TIPS WHEN FILING A COMPLAINT

KEEP IT SIMPLE: Avoid rambling. Try not to include any unnecessary or irrelevant information.

BE POLITE: Avoid personal attacks or insulting comments about the doctor.

TYPE THE LETTER: A complaint that is easy to read is easier to investigate.

PROVIDE RELEVANT INFORMATION: Include copies of any records about your medical treatment if you have them.

"How Do I Find a Qualified Medical Malpractice Lawyer?"

Choosing a lawyer to represent you is an important but daunting task. The decision certainly should not be made on the basis of advertising alone. The Yellow Pages are filled with ads – all of which say basically the same thing.

You shouldn't even hire me until you have met me and decided that you trust that I can do a good job for you.

I believe there are certain questions to ask that will lead you to the best lawyer for your case—no matter what type of claim you have. You will have to invest a bit of your time, but that's OK because the decision as to who to hire as your lawyer is very important.

Medical Malpractice claims are extremely complicated and new court decisions are being released by courts across the country every day. I believe that by narrowly focusing my efforts I am better able to serve my clients. I believe that a lawyer simply cannot develop expertise in all areas of the law.

If you hire a lawyer who has never successfully handled a medical malpractice case, or who has only represented plaintiffs in automobile cases, you may not be in the best of hands.

I believe it is so important that you get into the right hands that I will give you the names and telephone numbers of other good medical malpractice lawyers in our area if we do not agree to accept your case.

Why do I give you the names of my competitors? Simple – I believe that we are all on the same side in representing innocent victims. These people are lawyers for whom I have a great deal of respect. It is my desire, above all else, that people with meritorious cases get into the hands of experienced trial lawyers.

"How Do I Find Out Who Is Good In My Area?"

REFERRAL:

Get a referral from a lawyer that you do know. He or she may know someone who practices in the area you need. Most of my medical malpractice cases come from referrals from other lawyers or from satisfied clients.

YELLOW PAGES:

The Yellow Pages can be a good source of names. However, remember that placing an ad in the Yellow pages does not necessarily mean the lawyer has experience with medical malpractice claims.

CASE SELECTION:

Make sure that the lawyer you hire is selective enough with his or her cases that your important case does not become just one more file in the pile.

BOOKS OR REPORTS:

Ask each lawyer if they have information like this book so you can find out more about the lawyers qualifications and experience before you walk in the door.

THINGS TO LOOK FOR:

Here are a few factors to look for and question your lawyer about. Not every lawyer will meet all of these criteria, but the significant absence of the following should be a big question mark.

EXPERIENCE:

Obviously, the longer you have been practicing a particular area of the law, the more you will know. I believe that experience is a big factor in most cases. Ask the lawyer if he or she has achieved any significant verdicts or settlements. The larger the verdicts and settlements achieved, the more likely the defendants will respect your lawyer. While no lawyer can guarantee the outcome of a case, I have had several cases that we have been able to resolve with multi-million dollar results.

RESPECT IN THE LEGAL COMMUNITY:

Does the lawyer teach other lawyers in Continuing Legal Education courses? For example, I have been invited to teach and to other lawyers at conferences in Nova Scotia, New Brunswick, Prince Edward Island, Ontario, and even Singapore.

MEMBERSHIP:

In the Atlantic Provinces Trial Lawyers Association, or the Association of Trial Lawyers of America (now called the American Association for Justice). I have been honored to have been elected, by my colleagues, President of the Atlantic Provinces Trial Lawyers Association.

PUBLICATION:

Has your lawyer written anything that has been accepted for publication at legal conferences or in academic journals? This is another sign of respect that the legal community has for his or her skills and experience. This book is just an example, but I have published many papers for the Atlantic Provinces Trial Lawyers Association,the Canadian Bar Association, the Canadian Institute and the International Bar Association.

.

What Happens After You Decide On A Lawyer?

It is important to know how your lawyer will keep you informed about the progress of your case. In my practice, we generally send a copy of every piece of correspondence and pleadings in the case to the client. We take time to explain the "pace" of the case and in what time frames the client can expect activity to take place.

I have a very strict policy about office communications. I do not take inbound calls without an appointment. This allows me to schedule blocks of time to devote to my clients. However, my office is happy to schedule telephone appointments and and assist wherever possible to keep you up to date on the status of your claim.

Our clients are invited to email me at any time. My office tries to return calls within 24 hours. Sometimes that's impossible, particularly if I am traveling or in trial.

If I can't call you back, one of my associate lawyers or my assistant will help you set up a specific "telephone appointment." You are also invited to make an appointment to come in at a time that is convenient to you.

Find out who will actually be working on your case. Some large personal injury firms have a staff of people that aren't even lawyers who are in charge of managing their clients' claims. In other firms, client files are handed off to junior lawyers in order to give them more experience.

Make sure that you and your lawyer have a firm understanding as to who will be handling your case on a day to day basis. There are a lot of things that go on with a case that do not require the senior lawyer's attention.

On the other hand, if you are hiring a lawyer because of his or her experience, make sure that that person is going to be in charge of your claim.

What Do I Do For You in a Medical Malpractice Claim?

COLLECT THE FACTS:

In order to determine whether you have a case, we must first gather all of the relevant medical records involved in your care. Once all of the records are received, we review them to see if, based upon our experience, it looks as though there is a provable case of medical malpractice (I go into more detail about what happens if I think the medical files have been altered in some way).

CONSULT EXPERTS

If the case looks like it has merit, medical experts in the appropriate specialty must be consulted and retained. Again, these experts must be of the opinion that the medical care received was substandard.

COLLECT MORE INFORMATION:

Once we have retained experts who are prepared to testify on your behalf, other records, including employment records and tax returns must be obtained. This information will help us prove the damages or financial losses that have been suffered due to the defendant's negligence.

Tasks in a "Typical" Medical Malpractice Claim

Here is a more or less complete list of the tasks I may be called to do in your case.

Remember that each case is different, and that not all of these tasks will be required in every case.

- Interview the client;

- Educate you about medical malpractice claims;

- Gather documentary evidence including medical records and hospital documents;

- Interview known witnesses;

- Collect other evidence, such as photographs of the injury itself;

- Analyze the legal issues, such as contributory negligence and informed consent;

- Talk to your doctors or obtain written reports to fully understand your condition;

- Analyze your insurance policy to see if any money they spent to pay your bills must be repaid;

- Analyze the validity of any liens on the case. Insurance companies, social assistance benefit plans and employers may each claim that they are entitled to all or part of your recovery;

- Obtain relevant medical literature to help determine whether malpractice was involved in your injury;

- Recommend whether an attempt should be made to negotiate the claim or whether suit shall be filed;

- Obtain nursing and expert review of your claim;

- If suit is filed, prepare the client, witnesses and healthcare providers for discovery examinations;

- Prepare written questions and answers and take the discovery examination of the defendant and other witnesses;

- Produce to the defendant all of the pertinent data for the claim, such as medical bills, medical records, and tax returns;

- Go to court to set a trial date;

- Prepare for trial and/or settlement before trial;

- Prepare the client and witnesses for trial;

- Organize the preparation of medical exhibits for trial;

- Organize the preparation of demonstrative exhibits for trial;

- Prepare for mediation;

- File briefs and motions with the court to eliminate surprises at trial;

- Take the case to trial with a jury or judge;

- Analyze the jury's verdict to determine if either side has good grounds to appeal the case;

- Make recommendations to the client as to whether or not to appeal the case [our retainer agreement does not obligate us to appeal]

Altered Medical Files: What happens when the records have been tampered with?

One of my favourite movies of all times is The Verdict with Paul Newman. I love the scene where he proves that the defendant doctor altered the medical files of the woman who was in a coma because of the doctor's negligence.

Altering medical records does not happen as often as it appears on television or in the movies. However, it happens enough that experienced medical malpractice lawyers develop a sense of when further investigation into the legitimacy of a medical record or chart is warranted.

Some "red flags" that I look for, based on past experience in other cases, that may indicate the possibility of altered medical records are:

- Crowding or squeezing entries above a signature, or between lines;

- Erasures, crossed out entries or white-out corrections;

- Changes in slant of handwriting;

- Use of different pens or computer typeface to write one entry;

- Notes on different dates written in the same colour ink;

- Notes in different colour ink in the same entry;

- A typed entry following handwritten entries, or vice versa;

- Missing originals replaced by photocopies;

- Entries that are self-serving;

- Half sheets instead of the usual size of document (page cut in half);

- Additional entries on the original document, not appearing on alleged copies;

- An unusually late date of dictation or transcription, designated at the bottom of a typed document;

- Any handwritten entry made by someone who erred significantly in treatment, at odds with the rest of the chart.

LESSONS LEARNED FROM PAST CASES:

Over the past 18 years, I have learned some lessons about how to detect when a medical file may have been altered.

In one case I was involved in the specialist's report that was received by my client's family physician did not have (exculpatory) handwritten notes that appeared in the report in the specialist's file. Lesson: Look for all copies of the record and compare them.

In one case the surgeon dictated three different versions of the operative report. The family doctor received the first version days after my client's surgery. After my client's condition deteriorated, he dictated a second version (which was found in the Hospital chart). After my client became comatose and was transferred to another hospital for corrective surgery he dictated a third version of the report which was in his office copy of my client's chart. Lesson: Get the records, and get them fast.

In a claim involving allegations of nursing negligence the nursing notes contained statements that the patient's condition had been communicated to the attending physician. However the date of the entry was for a day that the nurse in question wasn't working. Lesson: Compare staffing sheets/timecards with the medical chart to detect entries/notes by staff members that were not present/on duty that day.

In a claim involving a fatal overdose the nursing notes indicated that the deceased had received the proper dosage of medication. However, the medication administration records, which were not supplied by the hospital when the chart was originally requested, showed that the medication had been administered to the patient twice. Lesson: Compare the medication administration records with the nursing notes and physicians orders.

In an anesthesia negligence claim the anesthesiologist tore up the original anesthesia record and prepared a new record with different data. One of the nurses involved in the operation retrieved the original record and scotch taped it together. Lesson: Interview everyone, including retired employees.

In a birth injury claim two of the babies APGAR scores had been whited out and changed from a 0 to a 2 (normal).

In a fatality claim the deceased's blood pressure reading had been changed from 170/90 to 120/80 by using a different colour pen to alter the numbers 7 and 9. The change couldn't been seen on the photocopy of the patient's chart, but was reasonably obvious on examination of the original chart.

Whenever I have a reasonable suspicion that the medical files have been altered, I make an appointment to attend at the Hospital or the doctor's office to view the original chart.

The Legal Process in Medical Malpractice Cases

In most cases today, attempting to negotiate with the defendant before filing suit is a waste of time and effort. The C.M.P.A. uses pre-suit negotiation only to find out as much about you, your lawyer and your doctor as they can. It is my opinion that many lawyers waste precious time attempting to negotiate with the defendant before filing suit.

If I accept your case it is because we believe it has merit and you deserve a trial by jury. We will usually file your suit before negotiating so that if negotiations break down, we will be able to head toward a trial date as quickly as possible.

I believe that it is a dangerous practice to wait until the Statute of Limitations has almost expired before filing suit. While there are legitimate reasons for delaying filing suit, there is no excuse for waiting until the last moment to see if the defendant will settle your case.

The Discovery Examination is the Key to a Successful Malpractice Claim

Despite being called a discovery examination, a discovery is not a test. A discovery is part of the legal process. You are asked questions under oath and a Court Reporter records your answers and prepares a written transcript.

The purpose of a discovery, as the name suggests, is to learn (or discover) all there is to know about the other side's case. A discovery can have a significant affect on the outcome of your case.

Sometimes the Defendant's lawyer will pick out key questions from your discovery and ask you those questions at trial. If you answer is significantly different at trial, the lawyer will use your discovery transcript to attack your credibility.

The discovery process also gives the Defendant's lawyer a chance to see how you will perform as a witness.

SECRETS TO A SUCCESSFUL DISCOVERY EXAMINATION

The Defendants lawyer will try to get you to provide as much information as possible. Do not volunteer information! Although, that sounds easy to do, it is actually very difficult. But if you remember that the purpose of the discovery is to find out as much as possible about your case it will make it easier for you to remember not to volunteer information.

THE GOAL OF YOUR DISCOVERY:

Your goal at discovery is NOT:

1. To win your case;

2. To show emotions;

3. To convince the Defendants lawyer about how good your case is.

Your goal at discovery is simple: to complete the discovery without providing the Defendant with information that can hurt your case.

ALWAYS TELL THE TRUTH:

The one thing that can hurt a case more than anything else is if you do not tell the truth during your discovery.

A lawyer can win a case with bad facts but it is almost impossible to win a case when a Judge or Jury thinks that you are lying.

Telling the truth is not only the right thing to do; it is in your best interest in order to win your case.

LISTEN TO THE QUESTION:

Listen to the question. Answer only the question that is asked. Next to telling the truth, this is the most important rule to remember during your discovery. It is also the hardest rule to follow.

When you have been living with the effects of an accident for some time you assume that the other lawyer will ask you about the issues or facts that you think are important. You may not listen to the question that is actually being asked, which may lead to you providing more information than necessary.

Listen to the question. Answer only the question that is asked. For example if you are asked: "Do you know what time it is?" A proper answer is "Yes" or "No". A "bad" answer is to say: "Yes, it's 3:00."

Do not suggest the next question from your last answer. For example, if you are asked: "Did you go to work after the accident?" A proper answer is "Yes".

A "bad" answer is: "I went to work after the accident but I had to leave early". This will lead the Defence lawyer to ask about the reasons why you left work early.

DO NOT RUSH TO ANSWER THE QUESTION:

After the Defendant's lawyer asks you a question, pause before answering. Pausing gives you time to think about your answer.

DON'T VOLUNTEER INFORMATION:

Volunteering information is almost always a bad idea. Telling the truth does not mean volunteering truthful information that is not necessary to answer the question. Do not do the other lawyers work.

Clients will often volunteer information in an effort to show the other lawyer that they "don't have anything to hide". Resist the temptation to fill in the gaps or volunteer information.

Answer the question truthfully and directly, and then stop. If the question can be answered by "yes", you should simply answer: "Yes". You should NOT answer by saying: "Yes, but you may also want to know about …"

Do not volunteer to provide information. For example: "I don't know, but I can ask my husband/wife/employer…"

Do not volunteer to provide documents. For example: "If you want I can get a copy of my medical records."

If the Defendant's lawyer asks if you would be willing to provide documents or other information you can respond that you are willing to provide anything that your lawyer recommends that you provide.

There are many things about your case that you think are important and you want the other side to hear because you think it will help your case. It is almost always a bad idea to volunteer this information because it allows the Defendants lawyer the opportunity to prepare to refute the information at trial.

SPECULATION:

Do not speculate. Do not explain things unless you are asked to. Do not give examples unless you are asked to. Most answers should be short and to the point.

OBJECTIONS:

If the other lawyer asks a question that is inappropriate I will object. Unless the objection is based on privilege (confidential discussions between you and me as your lawyer) generally you will be allowed to answer the question.

UNDERSTAND THE QUESTION:

If you do not understand the question, you should ask the lawyer to restate the question. You are entitled to have it in a form that you understand. If you do not understand the question, or a term in the question, say so.

The answer to a question you do not understand is almost always wrong.

The answer to a question you do not understand can almost always hurt your claim.

PREPARATION:

Finally, while it is not necessary to prepare in order to tell the truth, preparation is very important in order to be able to fairly respond and answer the questions that you will be asked during your discovery.

The Defence Medical Exam

Whenever you place your mental or physical impairment at issue in a claim for compensation, the defendant has a right under our rules of court to require that you undergo a medical examination by a doctor of the defendant's choosing.

The examination is usually referred to by defence lawyers as an "independent" medical examination or I.M.E. Make no mistake; there is nothing "independent" about it!

A more accurate term is a Defence Medical Examination (D.M.E.).

The defendant must give you reasonable notice of the time and place of the examination and the name of the D.M.E. doctor as well as the scope of the evaluation.

The D.M.E. doctor must to provide a copy of the report to you (or your lawyer) within a reasonable time after the examination. In exchange, you are required to provide copies of all medical office treatment notes, lab reports, consultations etc. from every doctor who has examined or treated you for the injury or impairment you are now claiming.

In addition, most defendants will also ask you for a signed authorization so that other information may be obtained before your D.M.E. date. Do not sign anything without consulting with your lawyer.

The D.M.E. doctor may be subpoenaed to give testimony under oath during a discovery examination, and may testify and be cross-examined at trial. Therefore, it is extremely important to be properly prepared for the D.M.E. and understand the objectives of the examiner.

The D.M.E. is a physical examination by a medical doctor chosen by the defendant (or their insurer) for the purpose of providing medical information which can be used to defend your claim.

In theory, D.M.E.'s are intended to "clarify" complex medical issues. In practice, the D.M.E. is a tool paid for by the defendant help them to deny your claim for compensation.

The problem is that for the most part, doctors whose practice consists primarily of conducting D.M.E.'s are not "independent medical examiners" by any reasonable definition. They are usually hired to provide testimony that supports the defendant.

D.M.E. doctors may render opinions and conclusions outside their area of medical expertise. D.M.E. doctors may also assume the role of a disability claims investigator, paid by the defence, to provide documentation that hurts your claim.

For example, in a brain injury case I was recently involved with, the Defendant's lawyer hired a local neurologist to do a D.M.E. to determine if my client had a brain injury. The Defence neurologist's report not only contained opinions in the field of neurology, but also psychology, psychiatry, neuropsychology and orthopedic medicine. All in an effort to deny that my client had a brain injury.

Therefore, it is important to remember D.M.E. doctors are not concerned with your medical well being. They have a clearly defined agenda and strategy to help the defendant's lawyer with what appears to be, credible, objective medical opinion contrary to that of your primary care physician or family doctor.

Some D.M.E. doctors see their job as being to attack your credibility by assuming that your claim is a fraud that must be exposed. It is a great deal easier to attack your credibility, and the judgment of your doctor, than it is to ascertain medical restrictions and limitations preventing you from returning to work.

D.M.E. doctors are provided with all the medical information your lawyer previously sent to the defendant's lawyer.

The D.M.E. doctor takes instruction from the Defendant's lawyer. Therefore, the D.M.E doctor already knows the "opinion" of the defendant concerning your ability to work before you arrive for the evaluation.

Doesn't it seem reasonable to conclude the D.M.E. doctor may have already formed an opinion concerning your impairment? Especially when the defendant's lawyer is the one that hired them!

If you are not prepared for the D.M.E. your claim may be seriously damaged. Although the following suggestions won't guarantee that your claim will be successful, it will help prevent the defence doctors from unduly damaging your claim.

THE D.M.E. PROCESS: PREPARE YOURSELF

The doctor will likely conduct an interview before the medical examination. The doctor typically refers to the interview as "taking your medical history".

The purpose of the interview is to obtain facts and comments from you which may be used after the D.M.E. to show you are inconsistent with your responses. For example, if you say you can't use your hands or carry heavy objects, don't lift a large bag and drive a vehicle to the D.M.E.

Always use common sense. Remember, the defence may have arranged for video surveillance the day before, the day of, and the day after your D.M.E.

Whatever you tell the doctor about your physical capacity should be the same information you told the defendant if you gave a statement or what you testified to at discovery. It should also be the same as any observed activity should the company have you under surveillance before the exam.

Keep in mind when speaking with the doctor to answer only the questions asked, and then be quiet. Never volunteer or offer additional information other than what is asked. (Read the chapter on preparing for a discovery examination if you want some tips to prepare for the D.M.E.)

SEE YOUR FAMILY DOCTOR THE SAME DAY:

When you know the date and time of the evaluation, call your family doctor and make an appointment just after the D.M.E. Tell your doctor that the defendant has asked you to submit to a D.M.E.

THIS SECOND EXAMINATION SERVES TWO PURPOSES:

1. It provides documentation of your physical condition by your family doctor on the same day as the D.M.E. exam, and

2. Sometimes the D.M.E. doctor may be a little rough and cause you to swell or have pain. Tell your doctor if you have pain, swelling, or any other physical symptoms as a result of the D.M.E. The documentation of your own doctor may be extremely important when pointing out inconsistent and unreasonable conclusions made by the D.M.E. doctor.

STUDY YOUR MEDICAL RECORDS:

It is extremely important that you review all of your prior medical records and history of your present disability. One way in which the D.M.E. doctor may draw suspicion to your claim is to "catch" you in inconsistencies when you talk about your prior medical history.

A simple lapse of memory by not mentioning a particular doctor, or lab test you had in the past is sufficient for the D.M.E. doctor to conclude you are trying to hide something and your claim is fraudulent. No prior doctor visit or treatment should be left out of your history, as you will certainly be asked about it at the beginning of the exam. Study your medical records before your D.M.E. date.

REFRESH YOUR MEMORY WITH THE FOLLOWING INFORMATION:

- Chronological medical history;

- A statement of the nature and extent of your disability;

- The date you first stopped working and why;

- How your disability has affected your activities of daily living (personal hygiene, meal preparation, dressing and undressing, preparation of meals etc.);

- Restrictions and limitations given by all treating doctors; and

- A complete description of your treatment plan discussed previously with your family doctor or treating physician.

Only when you are well prepared for discussing your medical history, can you avoid the "traps" of giving an inaccurate or inconsistent medical history. Skilled D.M.E doctors will make a big deal of every omitted detail no matter how insignificant it may seem.

TAKE SOMEONE WITH YOU:

Never attend a Defence Medical Examination alone. On the day of the exam, do not take part in any strenuous physical activity. Remember that the defendant's lawyer may have requested surveillance. Leave your house with someone who can assist you during the exam, ask questions for you, and/or take notes of procedures during the exam. Always request that the person who comes with you be allowed to stay with you during the D.M.E.

Nova Scotia's rules of court do not require that the doctor allow you to have someone with you during the examination. Some D.M.E. doctors will allow you to have someone with you, some will object. If they object, we can use that fact to question the objectivity of the examination.

If you to wear leg braces, wear them to the exam. If you use a cane, bring it with you, and use it. Bring a camera with you and take a picture of any swollen body part at the D.M.E. doctor's office. For example, if the D.M.E. doctor writes in his report that "there was no swelling", the picture can show that the D.M.E. report is not correct.

Ask your companion to take notes and to watch how the D.M.E. doctor treats you during the examination. Take someone with you who is fairly assertive and who would not have a problem asking for a break if you become tired, or need something to drink. Your companion is there to look out for you during the exam, and document what took place.

WADDELL SIGNS

D.M.E. doctors use certain exams to trick you. One such test, referred to as Waddell signs, used by physicians to identify psychological factors in patients claiming back problems from trauma, chronic pain and fibromyalgia.

So-called "false positives" on these indicators may be used against you by the D.M.E. doctor. The D.M.E. doctor will perform a hands-on examination for each test, looking for you to say "it hurts" when in fact it is impossible, given nerve or sensory distribution for it to really cause pain.

In other words, the D.M.E. doctor tries to "trick you" into saying it hurts when it really shouldn't, given the injury or diagnosis you have.

WADDELL SIGNS IN A NUTSHELL

TENDERNESS:

The doctor will lightly touch or pinch your skin over a wide area beyond the normal distribution of the sensory nerves. If you say these light touches are sensitive and tender, the D.M.E. doctor will suspect exaggeration. If you say you have pain when deeply touched over a wide area beyond the area of an injury or joint, the doctor will suspect exaggeration. Usually pain is only evident in the localized area of the injury. If you have fibromyalgia and say you have pain "everywhere", the doctor will suspect your reactions.

STIMULATION TESTS:

If the doctor presses down on your head while you are standing (this is called axial loading), and you report low back pain, the doctor will say you are exaggerating. If the doctor rotates your shoulders and pelvis at the same time while you are standing, and you complain of low back pain, the doctor will say you are exaggerating.

DISTRACTION TESTS:

Occasionally when the D.M.E. physician finds something wrong, the doctor may try to distract you, performing another test of the same area without telling you why. If you have a negative reaction, or don't give a full effort, the doctor will suspect exaggeration.

An example of this is to ask the patient to raise one leg against resistance while lying down. If your opposite leg does not press down, for leverage, then the doctor will suspect you are not giving full effort for the purpose of exaggeration.

Sometimes, the D.M.E. doctor will just walk away from you supposedly to write something down in your chart, and then quickly ask you a question. If you "turn your head" in the doctors direction when you said you couldn't do that because of pain, the doctor will suspect all of your complaints.

REGIONAL DISTURBANCES:

If you complain of excessive weakness of muscles within a particular group the doctor may say you are exaggerating. Likewise, if you claim numbness, tingling or pain over an area outside of where the nerves from the spine lead down the leg into the toes, the doctor may suspect exaggeration. This is especially true for fibromyalgia and chronic fatigue claims.

OVERREACTION:

If you cringe, grimace or otherwise show unnatural responses to sensory, motor or reflex tests (all of the above), the doctor may suspect exaggeration.

Other Types of Defence Medical Examinations

NEUROPSYCHOLOGICAL EXAMINATION

A neuropsychological exam uses scientifically validated tests to evaluate brain functions from simple motor performance to complex reasoning and problem solving. The results of these tests are then compared with normative standards.

While C.T. scans, M.R.I.'s, E.E.G.'s and P.E.T. scans identify structural, physical, and metabolic conditions of the brain, the neuropsychological examination is generally accepted by the medical community to be the only way to formally assess brain function.

MOST NEUROPSYCHOLOGICAL TESTS EXAMINE THE FOLLOWING:

- Attention and processing speed;

- Intelligence;

- Motor performance;

- Language skills;

- Sensory acuity calculation;

- Working memory;

- Vision analysis;

- Learning memory;

- Problem solving;

- Abstract thinking and judgment;

- Mood and temperament; and

- Executive functions

THE MALINGERING TEST (ARE YOU FAKING IT)?

The MMPI-2 (Minnesota Multiphasic Personality Inventory) is a well-known test designed to identify if a patient is exaggerating or faking their symptoms: "malingering." The test is frequently used by D.M.E. doctors.

OTHER COMMON TESTS USED DURING A NEUROPSYCHOLOGICAL EXAMINATION INCLUDE:

- The Beck Depression or Anxiety Scales (which provide a quick assessment of symptoms related to depression or anxiety);

- The Bender Visual Motor Gestalt test (evaluates visual-perceptual and visual-motor functioning and possible signs of brain dysfunction, emotional problems, and developmental maturity);

- Dementia Rating scale, (provides measurement of attention, initiation, construction, conceptualization, and memory to assess cognitive status in older adults with cortical impairment);

- Halstead Category test, (measures concept learning, flexibility of thinking and openness to learning. It is considered a good measure of overall brain function.)

There are other tests available to neurologists who generally select a combination of tests for each individual based on their diagnosis and history.

In order to be valid, neuropsychological examination results should be interpreted by a certified neuropsychologist, or psychologist. The neuropsychological tests are subject to interpretation, and of course, D.M.E. doctors often interpret the results in favour of the defendant.

Neuropsychological D.M.E.'s should not be used for all impairments, but because of the possible subjective nature of the interpretation, defendants sometimes request these exams because they can get results favorable to the defendant.

Neuropsychological exams should not be used in cases where the diagnosis is depression or other mental and nervous disease. Some tests may be applied in a psychological D.M.E., but using a neuropsychological exam alone to determine Axis I-IV diagnosis may not be appropriate.

FUNCTIONAL CAPACITY EXAMINATIONS

For structural injuries to the hands, bones, feet, and back and for chronic pain and fatigue issues, an F.C.E. administered by a qualified occupational therapist or doctor can produce objective, verifiable, and accurate results. Functional capacity examinations should be the most common type of D.M.E., unfortunately they are not.

Functional capacity evaluations include physical tests to determine how much weight you can lift or carry; your ability to use hands and feet (pinch strength, grip, manipulation); your ability to climb stairs, lift overhead, crawl, bend, stoop; your physical endurance, i.e. ability to work consistently and give full physical effort.

In Nova Scotia, F.C.E.'s are generally conducted by occupational therapists (O.T.) that have been trained to properly administer, and interpret, the tests. The O.T. will attempt to categorize your functional capacity by defining your physical ability as either:

- Sedentary;

- Light;

- Medium; or

- Heavy capacity.

The F.C.E. may result in a rating of full body disability usually expressed as a percentage. The defendant will ask the O.T. to give you restrictions and limitations (things you may not do at all, and activates you may only perform at a certain level or duration).

The O.T. will state whether he/she believes you made a full effort on the exam. As I mentioned earlier these evaluations are more reasonable and produce better results for both the defendant and for the injured person.

GAF RATINGS

Global Assessment of Functioning (G.A.F.) ratings are used to show to what extent a person's injuries or illness impact on their ability function on a day to day basis.

The GAF Scale in a Nutshell

100-91

Superior functioning in a wide range of activities, life's problems never seem to get out of hand, is sought out by others because of his or her many positive qualities. No symptoms.

90-81

Absent or minimal symptoms (e.g., mild anxiety before an exam), good functioning in all areas, interested and involved in a wide range of activities, socially effective, generally satisfied with life, no more than everyday problems or concerns (e.g., an occasional argument with family members).

80-71

If symptoms are present, they are transient and expectable reactions to psychosocial stressors (e.g., difficulty concentrating after family argument); no more than slight impairment in social, occupational, or school functioning (e.g., temporarily falling behind in schoolwork).

70-61

Some mild symptoms (e.g., depressed mood and mild insomnia) OR some difficulty in social, occupational, or school functioning (e.g., occasional truancy, or theft within the household), but generally functioning pretty well, has some meaningful interpersonal relationships.

60-51

Moderate symptoms (e.g., flat affect and circumstantial speech, occasional panic attacks) OR moderate difficulty in social, occupational, or school functioning (e.g., few friends, conflicts with peers or co-workers).

50-41

Serious symptoms (e.g., suicidal ideation, severe obsession rituals, frequent shoplifting) OR any serious impairment in social, occupational, or school functioning (e.g., no friends, unable to keep a job).

40-31

Some impairment in reality testing or communication (e.g., speech is at times illogical, obscure, or irrelevant) OR major impairment in several areas, such as work or school, family relations, judgment, thinking, or mood (e.g., depressed person avoids friends, neglects family, and is unable to work; child frequently beats up younger children, is defiant at home, and is failing at school).

30-21

Behavior is considerably influenced by delusions or hallucinations OR serious impairment, in communication or judgment (e.g., sometimes incoherent, acts grossly inappropriately, suicidal preoccupation) OR inability to function in almost all areas (e.g., stays in bed all day, no job, home, or friends).

20-11

Some danger of hurting self or others (e.g., suicide attempts without clear expectation of death; frequently violent; manic excitement) OR occasionally fails to maintain minimal personal hygiene (e.g., smears feces) OR gross impairment in communication (e.g., largely incoherent or mute).

10-1

Persistent danger of severely hurting self or others (e.g., recurrent violence) OR persistent inability to maintain minimal personal hygiene OR serious suicidal act with clear expectation of death.

0

Inadequate information.

Nine Tips to Help Prepare for your D.M.E.

1. Prepare for the D.M.E. in advance. Know your medical history and be consistent when telling your history to the D.M.E. doctor.

2. Let your family doctor know you have been asked to submit to a D.M.E. Make an appointment to be examined by your own doctor on the same day.

3. Take someone with you to the exam that can take accurate notes of the procedures. Take pictures of any swelling or obvious physical marks in the D.M.E. doctor's office.

4. Do not exaggerate symptoms or over react when touched or prodded.

5. Remember the D.M.E. doctor is not your friend or your medical doctor. Do not ask medical questions about your treatment, and answer only the questions you are asked.

6. Remember you may be watched by a private investigator. Wear braces, use canes, or other therapeutic devices

as instructed by your doctor. Limit your activities on the day before, the day of, and the day after your D.M.E. examination.

7. Ask for a copy of the D.M.E. report. The doctor may or may not give it to you, but ask anyway.

8. Stay calm, and if the D.M.E. physician hurts you, say so. If the D.M.E. doctor manipulates you, or physically hurts you to the point of pain, ask for an ambulance to be called.

9. After the exam, go home and relax. Be confident that whatever conclusion the Defendant's draw from the D.M.E. report, has nothing to do with you, or how you presented yourself during the exam.

"So How Long Does All of This Take?"

You can expect the legal process to take two to four years to complete. Some cases resolve sooner than that, but I will only accept cases from clients who are prepared to take the time we need to fully prepare their claim. I do not have the time to take cases from clients who are simply looking to settle quickly in order to "make a quick buck."

Why Should You Hire Me?

There are many lawyers who advertise for medical malpractice cases. There are capable experienced lawyers in this field, but it is difficult for a client to separate the good from the bad. You need to ask your lawyer all of the questions I have outlined in this report.

Our clients get personal attention because we are very selective in the cases that we take. We decline hundreds of cases a year in order to devote personal, careful attention to those few that we accept. We do not make money by accepting many small cases hoping to get a small fee out of each.

What Cases Do I Not Accept?

Because of the tremendous difficulty in obtaining a fair recovery in a medical malpractice case, most experienced malpractice lawyers will not accept a medical malpractice case unless there are significant financial damages at stake. Our court system is simply not set up to handle "small" medical malpractice cases.

Due to the high volume of calls and referrals from other lawyers that I receive, I have found that the only way to provide personal service is to decline those cases that do not meet my strict criteria.

These cases are expensive and time consuming. I would like to represent everyone who needs a good lawyer, but we cannot. Therefore, I generally do not accept the following types of cases:

- I do not accept cases where there is no evidence of a significant injury which was directly caused by the health care provider's malpractice.

- I do not accept cases where there is a significant pre-existing injury in the same body part. If you have had three back surgeries in the past and now claim that your most recent surgery is the cause of your chronic back pain, the chances of a jury awarding you a substantial amount of money is just about nil. Again, I feel that it is not worth the risk to the client to pursue these cases.

- I do not accept cases where the statute of limitations will soon run out. I like to have at least four months to adequately investigate and evaluate your claim. Your delay is not going to become my crisis.

"ARE THERE ANY CASES LEFT?"

Yes, there are, and that's just the point. We are a small firm and accept a limited number of cases each year.

We concentrate our efforts on increasing the value of good cases—not filing and chasing frivolous ones.

I only represent clients that I believe to have valid claims. When I devote my time and resources to representing only legitimate claimants with good claims, I am able to do my best work.

"HOW DO YOU DECIDE WHICH CASES YOU WILL TAKE?"

It normally takes months of work, research and investigation before I am able to decide if I will agree to represent a client in a medical malpractice claim.

COLLECTING AND REVIEWING THE MEDICAL RECORDS:

The first step of the review process is to collect all of the relevant records and information about the medical treatment that you (or your loved one) received. This includes getting copies and reviewing all of your hospital records as well as the records from your family doctor and any specialists that may have treated you for your injuries.

The cost of photocopying these records can sometimes amount to a couple of hundred dollars. My clients are responsible for paying for the cost of photocopying the records. Sometimes they are reluctant to incur that expense. In those rare cases, I have to tell the client that if the thought of risking $200.00 in order to find out if they have a legitimate medical malpractice claim scares them, then they are not ready for the kind of risks that a medical malpractice lawsuit will carry.

After we have collected all the relevant medical information, I review your records to see if, based on my past experience, there are any obvious medical-legal issues that may provide the grounds for a medical malpractice claim.

In some cases it is obvious after my initial review of the medical information that a medical malpractice claim is, or is not, likely to be successful.

I do not charge a fee for my initial review of your medical records.

MEDICAL SCREENING OPINION:

After I review all of your relevant medical records, I have a medical specialist review the chart to point out any medical issues of concern and to make recommendations about what specific medical specialists we will need to retain (hire) in order to testify for you in court. There is no charge for the medical screening.

HIRE AN EXPERT(S) FOR A MEDICAL LEGAL OPINION

If my review of your records indicates that there is a potential legal claim, and the medical screening indicates there are legitimate medical concerns that suggest there may have been malpractice in your medical treatment, then I recommend hiring a top notch medical expert who will testify for you if your claim goes to court.

I conduct a search throughout Canada and the United States to find an expert (or experts) who will be willing to review your medical chart, provide us with a medical legal opinion, and testify for you if the claim goes to trial.

I do not charge a fee for the time involved in searching for the medical expert.

Depending on the type of medical specialist that your claim requires, the cost of having the medical expert review your medical chart and provide us with a medical-legal opinion about the merits of your claim will usually be in the range of $1,000.00 and $3,000.00.

The client is responsible for paying for medical expert's medical-legal opinion. This expense sometimes scares some of my clients. But I have been told by many of the clients that I have represented in the past that the expense is worth it, because they finally get an answer to the question: "was the doctor who treated me (or my loved one) negligent?"

If an independent medical expert says that there was no negligence in my client's medical treatment then they have the peace of mind of knowing that they have done everything they can to investigate what happened to them, and to pursue all of their options.

MAKE AN INFORMED DECISION TO PROCEED:

If the medical expert determines that there was negligence, in your care or treatment, then you can make an informed decision about whether to proceed with a medical malpractice lawsuit.

Given the financial risk that my clients undertake it is my professional obligation to take on claims where I am confident that there was medical malpractice and that my clients have a reasonable chance of proving their claim in court. I will not take on cases that I do not think are legitimate in the hope of getting a quick settlement.

WE TAKE ON THE RISK OF THE LAWSUIT:

When I take on a medical malpractice lawsuit we carry all the legal fees and pay the costs and expenses associated with your lawsuit.

The cost of the medical experts alone for a typical medical malpractice lawsuit usually runs tens of thousands of dollars.

In other words, we are aware of the risks that you take when they file a medical malpractice lawsuit because we share those risks with you!

What Cases Will I Accept?

Given the tremendous expense of medical malpractice claims, we will not accept a case unless we believe that either the monetary losses (medical bills and lost wages, for example) are more than $100,000.00 or you have suffered a significant and permanent disability or disfigurement.

I WILL CONSIDER REPRESENTING YOU OR YOUR FAMILY IF:

- You or your family member suffered a serious or significant injury.

- You have been left with a permanent disability or serious disfigurement.

- Your family member has died because of the health care provider's negligence.

- You can no longer work because of your injuries.

- You can work, but your injuries reduce or limit your ability to earn an income.

- You have significant ongoing expenses for medical treatment.

- You are willing and able to pay for the cost of photocopying your medical records.

- You are willing and able to pay the cost of hiring a medical expert for a medical-legal opinion to make sure you have a legitimate claim.

Sometimes it is immediately clear that the injuries are going to meet my case selection criteria. It is easier to determine if someone has a potential claim when their family member has died, or if they have been left partially paralyzed, brain injured or have lost a limb or suffered serious fractures or a head injury.

However, in most cases in the days following medical treatment it is not immediately apparent what the future will hold. Will you fully recover after a few days or weeks, or will your injuries result in long term disability? In those cases I will consult with you and we determine the best course of action.

When I devote my time and resources to representing only legitimate claimants with good claims, I am able to do my best work. I have found that getting "bogged down" in lots of little cases, is not good for my clients with legitimate claims.

WHAT CAN YOU DO FROM HERE?

The most important thing that you can do as a potential medical malpractice plaintiff is to get a complete copy of all your hospital records. Any lawyer that represents you will need to have as complete a record as possible.

Keep a journal of events, and note the date, time, and circumstances of your developing situation.

Details are very important—malpractice cases may involve looking back at years of the patient's medical history, particularly if the defendant's lawyer argues that your injury was a result of a preexisting medical condition, rather than from malpractice.

You should already have started to look for experienced counsel to represent you in your case. It is likely that the statute of limitations in your province has already started to run. The legal process takes time—you should weigh your options for counsel carefully, but you should begin your search immediately.

OUR SERVICES

Sometimes the best advice I can give is that you do not have a claim that can be won. If that is true, I will tell you. If your case meets my criteria for acceptance, you can be assured that you will receive my personal attention. I will keep you advised as to the status of your case and give you my advice as to whether your case should be settled or whether we should go to trial. If we go to trial, I will be the lawyer trying your case.

My initial consultation is free. I will fully explain all fees and costs to you before proceeding. Together, as a team, you and

I will decide on the tactics best suited for your case. I look forward to hearing from you.

I hope you have found this information to be helpful. If you would like to discuss your claim with me, you can call me at 902-423-2050 or toll-free in the Atlantic Provinces at 1-877-423-2050.

JOHN A. MCKIGGAN

306-5670 Spring Garden Road
Halifax, NS B3J 1H6

Office: 902-423-2050
Fax: 902-423-6707
Toll-Free: 877-423-2050

www.apmlawyers.com

WA